Poinsettia

Star of Bethlehem

Poinsettia

Mistletoe, Holly, Pinecones and Needles

Holly

Christmas Rose

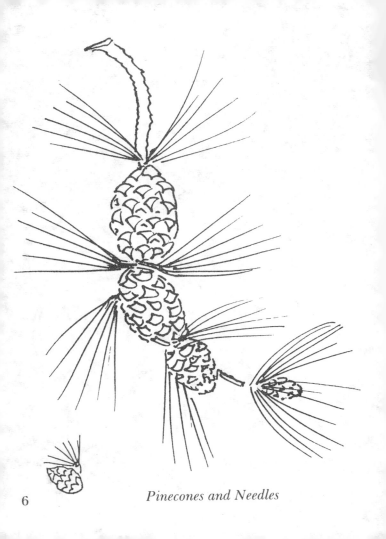

Pinecones and Needles

Carnation

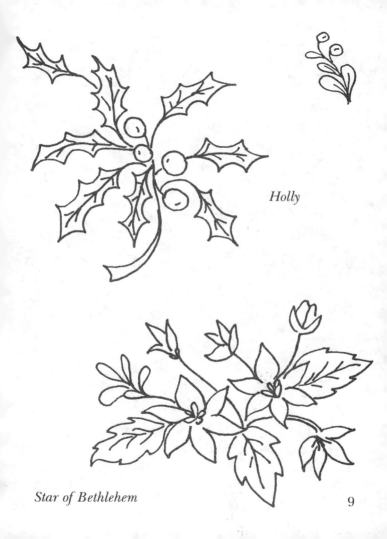

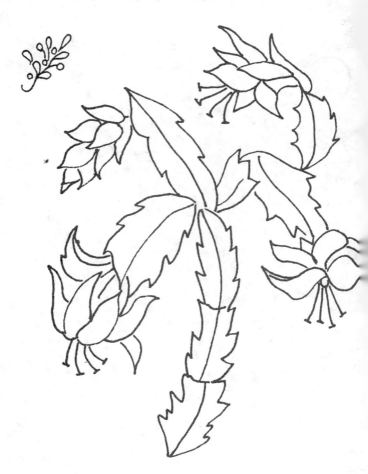

Christmas Cactus

Mistletoe

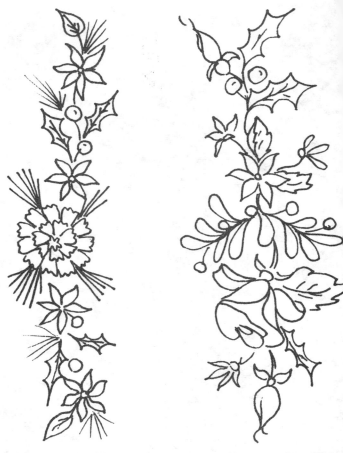

Carnation, Star of Bethlehem, Holly, Pine

Rose, Holly, Star of Bethlehem, Mistletoe

Christmas Cactus, Mistletoe

Christmas Rose

Pinecones and Needles

Star of Bethlehem

Christmas Rose with Holly